WITHDRAWN

D0849428

Volcanoes
in Our
Solar System

Volcanoes
in Our
Solar System

G. Jeffrey Taylor

Illustrated with photographs and drawings

87-357

DODD, MEAD & COMPANY · NEW YORK

551.2
Tay

ACKNOWLEDGMENTS

The author thanks Klaus Keil, Al Rubin, and Carl Allen for helpful hints on the manuscript, and the staff of the National Space Science Data Center for their efficient cooperation in supplying photographs from NASA missions to the planets.

ILLUSTRATION CREDITS: Carl Allen, 26-27, 27 (bottom); Lick Observatory, 36; NASA, EROS Data Center, 25, 29; NASA, Johnson Space Center, 11, 47 (top), 87; National Space Science Data Center, 17, 20, 39, 40, 41, 43, 45, 46, 51, 52-53, 56, 66, 68, 69, 70, 71, 72-73, 76, 82, 84; Keith Ronnholm, 8; Judy Salas, 14, 15, 16, 31, 32, 78; Soviet Academy of Sciences, 62; G. Jeffrey Taylor, 22, 47 (bottom), 79; U.S. Geological Survey, 60.

Library of Congress Cataloging in Publication Data

Taylor, G. Jeffrey, date
    Volcanoes in our solar system.

    Includes index.
    Summary: Explores the phenomenon of volcanism as it
occurs throughout our solar system on planets,
asteroids, and moons.
    1. Solar system—Juvenile literature. 2. Planets—
Geology—Juvenile literature. 3. Volcanism—
Juvenile literature. [1. Solar system. 2. Volcanoes]
I. Title.
QB501.3.T38 1983   551.2'1'0999   82-19819
ISBN 0-396-08118-5

For R. V. Fodor, who rekindled my interest in writing.

Contents

1 Volcanoes in Our Solar System   9

2 Planets, Moons, and Asteroids: A Guide to the
      Solar System   13

3 Earth: Active Volcanoes and Moving Plates   21

4 Earth's Moon: Samples of Ancient Lava Flows   35

5 Mercury: Old Volcanic Plains   50

6 Venus: Large Volcanoes—and Maybe Active Ones   57

7 Mars: The Largest Volcanoes in the Solar System   65

8 Asteroids and Meteorites: The Oldest Lava Flows   75

9 Io: Many Active Volcanoes   83

10 Searching for More Volcanoes   86

    Glossary   90

    Index   93

Mount St. Helens, Washington, only fourteen seconds after it began to erupt on May 18, 1980.

1 Volcanoes in Our Solar System

Volcanoes have fascinated, awed, and terrified people for all of human history. These exploding mountains have been sources of superstition, objects of scientific study, and sculptors of scenic landscapes.

About five hundred active volcanoes dot Earth's surface. In May, 1980, one of these, Mount St. Helens, reminded citizens of Washington and Oregon that it was anything but a dormant, peaceful peak among the majestic Cascade Mountains. Mount St. Helens erupted violently, killing about seventy people. It exploded with the force of 10 million tons of TNT (a high explosive) and blasted out a little more than half a cubic mile (2½ cubic kilometers) of ash and rock.

As impressive as this eruption was, it was tiny compared to others that have occurred during recorded history. In 1815, for example, the Tambora volcano on the Indonesian island of Sumbawa dumped forty times as much ash as did Mount St. Helens and it killed twelve thousand people.

All this volcanic activity proves that Earth is a geologically active planet. By studying volcanic rocks scientists try to learn about the processes operating deep within our planet, how mountains form, and why volcanoes erupt where they do. In short, the study of volcanoes teaches scientists how our planet works.

But Earth is not the only place where volcanoes occur. Earth's moon experienced a period of volcanism from 3 to 4 billion years ago. The planet Mercury seems to have had a similar history. Venus has some large, apparently active volcanoes. Mars has the largest volcanoes in the solar system, though they no longer erupt. Some asteroids, chips of which have fallen to Earth as meteorites, had lava erupt onto their surfaces $4\frac{1}{2}$ billion years ago. Finally, the giant planet Jupiter has a moon named Io that is the most volcanically active body in the solar system.

Scientists study volcanoes on these planets as well as on Earth. In fact, we really cannot understand volcanism completely by investigating only how the process operates on Earth. That would be like trying to determine how the human body works by studying one person's body instead of many. We learn much more by comparing planets to one another than by studying just one of them.

Scientists also study volcanoes on other planets so they can learn more about Earth's early history. On our planet, geologic forces like rain, wind, floods, volcanism, and mountain building are so active that the record of geologic events that happened billions of years ago is missing. Although Earth is $4\frac{1}{2}$ billion years old, the oldest rocks are only $3\frac{1}{2}$ billion years old and more than two-thirds of Earth's surface is less than 200 million years

Lift-off of a Titan/Centaur rocket at the Kennedy Space Center in Florida, the beginning of the Voyager spacecraft's long journey to Jupiter, Saturn and beyond.

old. So, to find out what happened long ago when Earth was young, scientists study other planets.

For most of human history, scientists were unable to study volcanoes anywhere but on Earth. Fortunately, the space age changed that. It made it possible to study planets other than our familiar Earth. Instead of being rather uninformative specks of light in the night sky, the planets have become geological field areas that scientists can study in much better detail than they could before rockets blasted off Earth and spacecraft soared toward the other planets.

This book describes what planetary scientists have learned about volcanoes on Earth, on Earth's moon, Mercury, Venus, Mars, asteroids, and Jupiter's moon Io. These are the only places where volcanism either took place or is now occurring in the *explored* parts of the solar system. Spacecraft have not yet traveled close to Neptune, Uranus, Pluto, and their moons to find out if volcanoes exist on them.

2 Planets, Moons, and Asteroids: A Guide to the Solar System

The solar system consists of the sun and the objects that follow circular paths, or *orbits*, around it. These objects include nine planets, more than forty moons, and millions of asteroids. With all these objects circling the sun, you would think that the solar system is a crowded place. But it is not congested at all. The solar system is mostly empty space.

The emptiness arises because the sun and planets are tiny compared to the vast distances between them. To get a better idea of this, imagine the sun being the size of a basketball. At this scale, Jupiter, the largest planet, would be a little smaller than a golf ball and would orbit the sun at a distance of 500 feet (150 meters). Earth would be much closer to the sun, 100 feet (30 meters), but it would be only one-tenth the size of Jupiter, about the size of a pea.

The Sun—the Star of the Solar System
The sun is the biggest and brightest object in the solar system. In fact, the sun is about a hundred times larger than all the planets

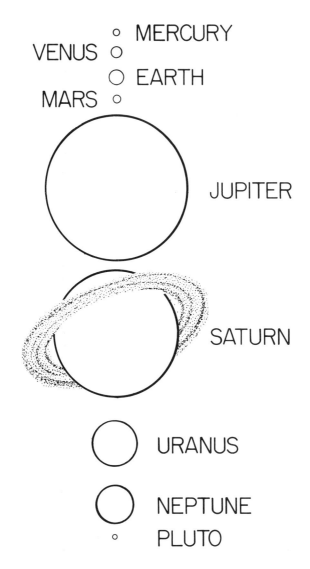

MERCURY
VENUS
EARTH
MARS
JUPITER
SATURN
URANUS
NEPTUNE
PLUTO

RELATIVE SIZES
OF THE PLANETS

This shows how the planets differ in size. They are, however, much farther apart than they appear in this diagram. Note how much larger the outer planets, especially Jupiter and Saturn, are compared to the inner ones.

combined. It is a star, much like the pinpoints of light that decorate the sky at night. Like the trillions of other stars in the universe, the sun consists of hot gases and produces light by nuclear fusion. During nuclear fusion, atoms of hydrogen, the lightest element, combine with each other to make atoms of helium, the next heavier element. This process releases tremendous amounts of energy, much of which ends up shining from the sun as visible light.

Planets—Some Rocky, Some Gaseous

Planets are bodies that orbit the sun. The planets closest to the sun (Mercury, Venus, Earth, and Mars) are made mostly of

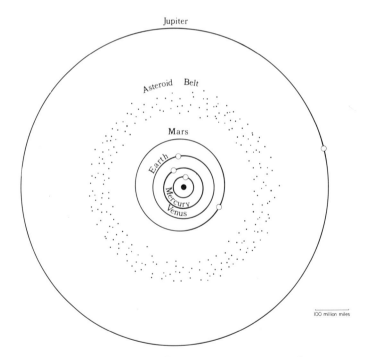

This diagram shows the relative distances of the inner planets from the sun. Each planet follows a circular path, or orbit, around the sun.

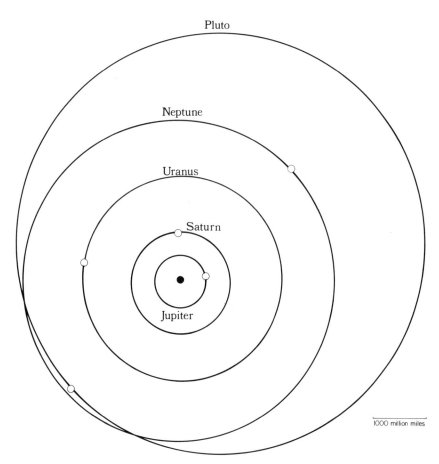

Pluto

Neptune

Uranus

Saturn

Jupiter

1000 million miles

The orbits of the outer planets. The inner planets all have orbits closer to the sun than Jupiter's orbit.

rock. Earth has a ball, or core, of metallic iron in its center. The core begins 1,800 miles (2,900 kilometers) beneath Earth's surface, about halfway to the center of the planet. A small portion of the core is solid iron, but most is molten iron, liquified by the intense heat in Earth's interior. Scientists believe that the other inner planets also have cores, but no one is sure how large the cores are or precisely what they are made of.

Most of the planets farthest from the sun (Jupiter, Saturn, Uranus, and Neptune) are giant bodies made mostly of hydrogen. The outer planets do not have volcanoes, but they do have small cores of rock and metallic iron. The cores are surrounded by liquid hydrogen. These giant planets are very different from small planets like the one we live on. Pluto, the farthest planet from the sun, is small and may be a mixture of rock and ice.

Moons—Companions of the Planets

Moons, or *satellites*, are small bodies that orbit a planet. Because the planets orbit the sun, the moons, of course, also orbit the sun,

Photograph of part of Jupiter, showing the giant Red Spot (swirly area in the lower left), which is a storm larger than Earth. Two of Jupiter's moons, Io (left, in front of the Red Spot) and Europa are also in view.

but they do so as they circle around a planet. Earth and Pluto each have one moon, Mars has two, Jupiter has fifteen, Saturn has seventeen, Uranus has five, and Neptune has two. Venus and Mercury do not have moons. As far as we know, only Earth's moon and Jupiter's moon Io have had volcanoes erupt on their surfaces.

Asteroids—Little Planets

Asteroids orbit the sun between Mars and Jupiter. The largest, Ceres, is 600 miles (1,000 kilometers) across. The smaller the size, the more numerous asteroids are. For example, there are about thirty asteroids larger than 125 miles (200 kilometers) across, more than two hundred asteroids larger than 60 miles (100 kilometers), and about two thousand bigger than 6 miles (10 kilometers) across. It is nearly impossible to see asteroids smaller than about a mile across, but scientists estimate that there are about 500,000 asteroids larger than a half mile (1 kilometer) and about 100 billion larger than 3 feet (1 meter) across. Although many of the billions of chunks of rock originated by collisions among the asteroids, they were never all part of one larger planet. The asteroid belt originated because the material in this area of the solar system never came together to form a planet.

Comets—Icy Inhabitants of the Outermost Solar System

Scientists know less about comets than any other type of body in the solar system. We know that comets are made mostly of ices (not only frozen water, but also frozen compounds of hydrogen, carbon, and nitrogen) and contain some rocky material.

Some scientists call them "dirty snowballs." No volcanic activity occurs on comets.

Comets follow long, slow paths around the sun. Their orbits are located beyond Pluto's and up to 5 *trillion* miles from the sun, and there may be up to 100 billion of them! Occasionally, one of these comets receives a gravitational nudge, perhaps from a passing star, and heads in toward the inner solar system. When it comes close to the sun, the comet heats up and glows as gases begin to escape from it. The closer it gets to the sun, the more spectacular the show. After rounding the sun, some comets leave the solar system and never return. Others follow long, skinny orbits that bring them close to the sun at regular intervals. Halley's comet, for example, returns to give earthlings a beautiful show every seventy-six years.

The Third Planet—a Special Place

The most pleasant planet is the third one from the sun. Called Earth, it is inhabited by creative and curious creatures called humans, like you and me, as well as by numerous plants and animals. Some of its human population have traveled to Earth's moon to study volcanic rocks there and others have sent automated spacecraft to study the other planets in the solar system. These efforts have paid off in giving Earth's inhabitants a solid understanding of the planets, moons, and asteroids in the solar system, including an understanding of where, when, and how volcanoes occur.

87-357

The planet Earth. The main landmass visible is Africa, which continental drift has caused to split from Arabia (near the top, center), enlarging the Red Sea and the Gulf of Aden.

3 Earth: Active Volcanoes
and Moving Plates

Volcanoes are produced when lava (molten rock) squirts out onto the surface of a planet or moon and piles up, forming a mountain. Lava does not always form a mountain, however; sometimes it simply oozes up along cracks and spreads out along the ground for great distances. Even when no mountain is built, geologists still refer to the outpouring of lava as "volcanic activity."

Volcanoes have several distinct shapes and they erupt with varying degrees of violence. The different shapes and styles of eruption are due mainly to the chemical compositions of the different types of volcanic lava.

Types of Volcanic Rocks
Geologists have identified many kinds of volcanic rocks but there are two main types. One, called *basalt*, contains more iron, magnesium, and calcium, and less silicon than the other type, called *andesite*. These differences in chemical composition cause basalt lava to be hotter when it erupts, 2,100°F (1,150°C), than is

Microscopic view of a thin slice of Earth basalt. The shapes of the minerals arise only when they crystallize in a lava flow. The white mineral is feldspar; the darkest is pyroxene. Actual area photographed is 8/100 inch (2 millimeters) across.

andesite lava, 1,800°F (1,000°C). Basalts are darker in color than andesites.

The different chemical composition results in basalt lava being able to flow much more easily than andesite lava, which is stickier, or more *viscous*. This is important because the more viscous a lava is, the harder it is for gas bubbles to escape to Earth's surface. Consequently, as the sticky andesite lava moves toward the surface, but is still beneath a volcano, the gas pressure builds up. The pressure finally becomes so great that it forces the lava up and out of the volcano in one, explosive event. The pressure builds up beneath a basalt volcano, too, but to a far lesser extent than beneath an andesite volcano. This explains why basalt eruptions are not so vigorous as andesite eruptions.

The difference in the ease with which basalt and andesite lavas flow also causes the volcanoes they form to have different shapes. Basalt volcanoes have slopes that are not as steep as andesite volcanoes because basalt lava flows greater distances, instead of building up around the vent.

What Volcanic Rocks Look Like

If you pick up a rock from a volcano and take it to a geologist, he or she will tell you that the rock is volcanic, even if you do not say where you collected it. This amazing feat is not accomplished because geologists are so smart (although they certainly are!), but because a rock formed by the solidification of lava has a distinctive appearance.

One of the obvious characteristics of volcanic rocks is that they contain small crystals (mineral grains). In many cases, you cannot see individual crystals without the aid of a magnifying glass. When viewed in a microscope, the crystals are arranged in distinctive patterns that are not observed in other types of rocks. The small size is due to the rapid rate at which lava flows cool. There simply is not enough time for large crystals to grow. Nevertheless, some volcanic rocks do contain larger crystals (called *phenocrysts*) surrounded by the usual small ones. These large crystals formed when the lava began to crystallize in large pools called *magma chambers* deep within Earth or as it traveled through Earth's crust on its long journey to the surface.

Many volcanic rocks have numerous holes in them. These holes, called *vesicles*, form when bubbles of gas are trapped as the lava solidifies. Some volcanic rocks have no vesicles; others (for example, *pumice*) have so many vesicles that they consist of more air than rock and can float on water.

Types of Volcanoes

The place where lava pours onto the surface of a planet is called a *vent*. If the vent is small, the volcanic material is deposited around it and a cone-shaped volcano forms. At the top of many volcanoes there is a circular, flat-floored· hole called a *crater*. *Calderas* are circular depressions much larger than volcanic craters. A caldera forms when the top of a volcano collapses. This occurs when lava had pooled underground but then erupted, leaving an empty chamber beneath the volcano. The volcanic rock is too weak to support the weight of the overlying rock and the top part of the volcano falls into the cavity. A caldera can also form when a volcano's top is blown off during an eruption.

Shield volcanoes are wide mountains with gently sloping sides. They are made of numerous solidified lava flows. Their shapes, which resemble the shields used by knights in armor, suggest that the lavas must have been able to flow easily; otherwise their slopes would be steeper. Knowing that basalt lava flows more easily than does andesite lava, it is not surprising that shield volcanoes are composed of basalts.

Shield volcanoes are large features. The island of Hawaii, for example, is built entirely of five shield volcanoes, which rise from the floor of the Pacific Ocean. The largest two, Mauna Loa and Mauna Kea, cover 2,900 square miles (7,600 square kilometers), about 75 percent of the island, and they reach heights of over 13,000 feet (4,100 meters). And this represents only the portions above sea level! Considering that the average depth of the ocean is over 12,000 feet (3,800 meters), it is obvious that these are immense mountains.

The *Emi Koussi, Africa, shield volcano*, as photographed by NASA's Landsat *satellite. The crater on top is a caldera and is 10 miles (16 kilometers) across. Compare this to shield volcanoes on Mars.*

Cinder cone near Flagstaff, Arizona.

Cinder cones are much smaller and steeper than shield volcanoes. They are composed mostly of rock fragments and drops of lava thrown out of a volcanic vent. The fragments and lava, called *pyroclastic* deposits, range in size from those smaller than about a quarter of an inch (half a centimeter) to those a few inches across. The drops of lava usually cool so fast that they do not crystallize and instead form glass. Cinder cones form from eruptions of either basalt or andesite lavas, and they tend to be small, rarely higher than about 500 feet (150 meters).

Composite volcanoes, like the Cascade Mountains in the northwestern United States, are the most majestic volcanoes. They are made of alternating layers of solidified andesite lava and pyro-

Below: *Mount Fujiyama, Japan, a composite volcano, is 12,385 feet (3,775 meters) high.*

clastic deposits. Their slopes are steeper than those of shield volcanoes, but not as steep as those of cinder cones. They can reach great heights above the surrounding terrain. The highest peaks in Oregon and Washington, for example, are composite volcanoes, as is the highest mountain in the Western Hemisphere, Mount Aconcagua in Argentina, which rises to 22,834 feet (6,960 meters) above sea level.

Sometimes sticky lava, andesite or even stickier types, solidifies at the vent of a volcano. This forms a *dome*, a mass of solidified lava with very steep sides. The formation of a dome can cause pressures to build up beneath it, frequently resulting in a massive eruption. This has happened at Mount St. Helens.

Large areas of Earth's continents are covered by lava flows that did not form volcanoes. These lavas were basalts that flowed easily from numerous vents and from long cracks called *fissures*. Because they cover such large areas, these flows are called *flood basalts*. They are also called *plateau basalts* because they frequently form large, flat areas known as plateaus. No flood basalts are erupting now. However, vast amounts of basalt lava erupt onto the ocean floor along the long, nearly continuous chain of underwater ridges known as the *mid-ocean ridge system*. Rapid cooling by ocean water prevents the lavas from flowing too far from their vents.

One of the most impressive deposits of flood basalts on a continent is the Columbia Plateau in parts of Washington, Oregon, Idaho, and northern California. An enormous volume of basalt covers about 76,000 square miles (200,000 square kilometers) and averages about 3,300 feet (1,000 meters) thick. Individual

Lava flows and volcanic craters in the Pinacate volcanic field, northern Mexico. The largest crater is 1 mile (1,600 meters) across.

flows range in thickness from about 10 feet (3 meters) to 100 feet (30 meters). Almost all this volcanic activity took place during a 3½-million-year period beginning 17 million years ago. Similar deposits occur in India, South America, South Africa, and other areas.

Locations of Active Volcanoes

Active volcanoes are not distributed uniformly around the world. Instead, they are concentrated in belts. The most prominent of these is the *circum-Pacific belt* (also called the "Pacific Ring of Fire"). This includes the west coasts of South and North America, Japan, the Philippines, Indonesia, and the Aleutian Islands in Alaska. Almost all of the volcanoes in these areas are composite volcanoes. Active basalt volcanoes occur as mid-ocean islands like Hawaii and along mid-ocean ridges.

This distribution of active volcanoes, which is matched by the distribution of earthquakes, is a fundamental fact about Earth. It can be explained by the theory of plate tectonics.

Moving Plates and Drifting Continents

Anyone who has examined a globe has noticed that South America and Africa appear to fit together as if they were pieces of a giant jigsaw puzzle. This observation, combined with detailed geologic investigations of continents and ocean basins, has led to the idea that South America and Africa were once pieces of a single large continent. This ancient continent split apart and the two new, smaller continents drifted away from one another. Further study has revealed that not only are the continents moving in relation to one another, but so are the ocean floors. Earth's

30

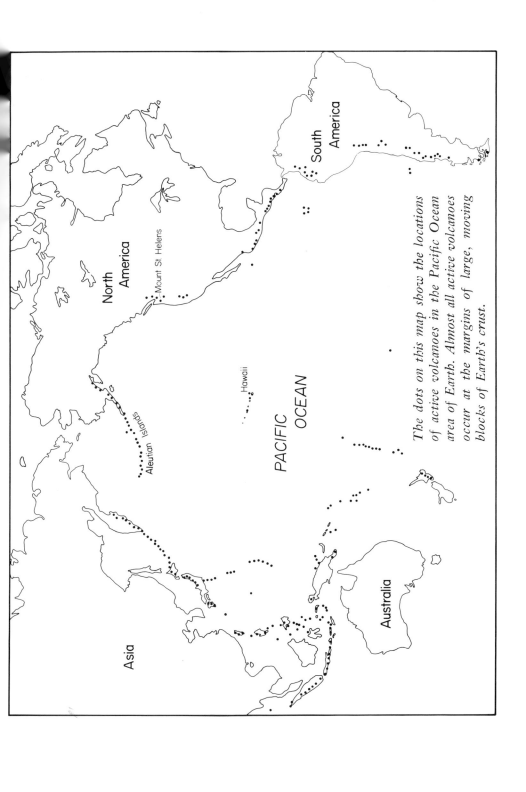

North
America

South
America

Mount St Helens

PACIFIC
OCEAN

Hawaii

Aleutian Islands

Asia

Australia

The dots on this map show the locations of active volcanoes in the Pacific Ocean area of Earth. Almost all active volcanoes occur at the margins of large, moving blocks of Earth's crust.

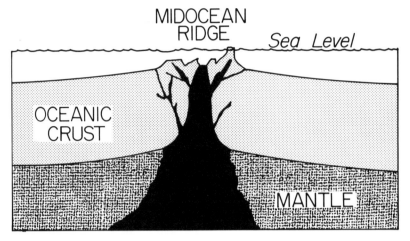

The lava (or magma when beneath the surface) generated at mid-ocean ridges is basalt (black in this diagram). It forms by partial melting of Earth's mantle.

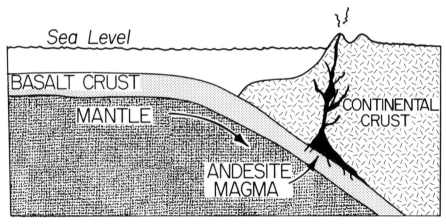

Where two crustal plates collide, one is dragged beneath the other. In these areas, the lava produced is andesite.

crust is broken into about six large, mobile blocks, or plates, and several smaller ones. Continents ride on these plates. The comprehensive theory that explains continental drift is called *plate tectonics*.

Almost all volcanic activity takes place at the boundaries of crustal plates. In some places, such as mid-ocean ridges, plates are moving away from one another. As they move apart, hot, but solid, rock from the interior slowly moves up along the mid-ocean ridges and begins to melt. In these cases, basalt lava erupts. Where plates collide, one plate dips beneath another. For example, along the west coast of South America, the Pacific Plate dives beneath the American Plate, dragging the ocean floor and part of the mantle with it. The rocks dragged down into the hotter regions of Earth begin to melt and andesite lava forms.

Some volcanoes occur in the middle of plates. A good example is Hawaii. In this case and for most mid-plate volcanoes, the lava formed is basalt. Flood basalts also appear to be in the middle of plates, but they probably were near plate edges when the lavas formed millions of years ago. Many scientists believe that flood basalts erupted when the crust began to pull apart, but for some reason did not move too far.

Where and How Lava Forms
Earth is much hotter inside than it is outside where we live. The fact that red-hot lava pours out from the planet's interior is solid evidence that Earth must be hot inside. Most lava forms in the mantle, the major zone of Earth that is located beneath the crust. In areas within Earth where the temperatures are hotter than the

melting point of the rocks composing the mantle, melting occurs, forming *magma*. (Magma is simply lava that has not reached the surface.) Because the minerals in mantle rocks have different melting temperatures, the magma thus formed has a chemical composition different from that of the rock that began to melt and is either like basalt or andesite, depending on where the melting takes place.

Once some magma has formed it begins to collect and moves along cracks and other weak zones toward the surface. If the magma never erupts, but instead solidifies at depth in Earth, it forms *intrusive* rocks. Intrusive rocks contain much larger crystals than do volcanic rocks. Examples are *gabbro* (if the magma was of basalt composition) and *granodiorite* (if of andesite composition). Another common type of intrusive rock is *granite*, which contains more silicon and less iron and magnesium than andesite.

The details of magma formation are complicated and many geologists are working hard to figure them out. It is important research because the lavas we sample at volcanoes come from inside Earth, and, therefore, contain information about the types of rocks that occur deep within our planet.

4 Earth's Moon: Samples of Ancient Lava Flows

Scientists know more about the Moon than about any other body in the solar system, except Earth. This knowledge has been gained by astronomers spending long, frequently cold, and lonely nights observing the Moon through telescopes mounted in observatories on Earth; by astronauts and automated spacecraft photographing the lunar surface as they orbited the Moon; and by scientists studying rocks collected by astronauts as they walked on the desolate lunar surface.

Rugged Old Highlands and Smooth Plains
There's a rabbit on the Moon and a man in the Moon, depending on how you look at it. These familiar, though vague, shapes appear because of entirely accidental arrangements of the two major types of terrain on the Moon. One is light colored, rugged, and higher than the other, which is relatively dark and smooth.

The light-colored areas are called the lunar *highlands*. They are rough because they were bombarded with enormous meteorites, some almost a hundred miles (160 kilometers) across and

Earth's moon. Darkest areas are lava flows, most of which fill giant meteorite-impact craters. Lighter areas are the heavily cratered highlands, which contain few volcanic rocks. Light streaks are rays, material thrown out of relatively young impact craters.

plenty of them several miles across, traveling at many thousands of miles per hour. Such large and fast objects do incomprehensible damage to the surface they hit and destroy much of the geologic information about the Moon before the impact. Nevertheless, painstaking work by scientists demonstrates that most of the rocks in the highlands are not volcanic. Instead, they formed when magmas crystallized at depth in the Moon, not on the surface.

The dark areas are called *maria*. "Maria" is the Latin word for "seas." These dark areas reminded Galileo of the sea when he looked at the Moon through one of the first telescopes ever made. That was in 1610 and he had made the telescope himself. We now know that the maria are not seas or oceans at all. They are composed of lava flow upon lava flow. Let's look at the maria in more detail. (The highlands are just as interesting to scientists as the maria, but because they contain few volcanic rocks, we will not consider them in this book about volcanoes.)

The Dark Lava Plains: the View from Orbit

A curious fact about the maria is that they are located almost entirely on one side of the Moon. This side is the one that we always see from Earth. The other side of the Moon is adorned with only a few patches of maria.

There are no active volcanoes on the Moon. All we see when looking down from a spacecraft orbiting the Moon are the results of geologic events that took place in the distant past. There are countless craters, but these are not calderas—volcanic craters caused by the collapse of the top of a volcano. The craters on the Moon were formed when meteorites struck the surface and blasted out holes. Scientists can distinguish impact craters from calderas because impact craters have rims that rise above the surroundings. The raised rim results when rocks are thrown out of the craters. In contrast, calderas have no debris piled up around them because they form by collapse. In other words, an impact crater forms by a hole being dug and the debris thrown out, but a caldera forms when rock falls into a hole within a volcano.

The most abundant volcanic features on the Moon are flood basalts. The maria are composed of countless lava flows that fill ancient, gigantic meteorite impact craters. The total thickness of solidified lava averages about 1½ miles (2 kilometers). The fronts of lava flows appear as curved cliffs, or *scarps*. Like the flood basalts in Oregon and Washington, those on the Moon flowed great distances. In some cases, individual lava flows dribbled across the Moon's surface for hundreds of miles. This indicates that the lavas must have been able to flow easily and so are more like basalt than andesite. Studies of Moon rocks from the maria confirm that the lavas were basalt.

There are no composite volcanoes on the Moon and few, if any, shield volcanoes. There are, however, other features that are probably volcanic. The most interesting are called *rilles*. These are long valleys that sculpture the surfaces of the maria. Some are straight and others follow irregular, curving paths, resembling rivers on Earth. Neither type formed by flowing water, however.

Lava flows are visible in this photograph of Mare Imbrium, the largest of the lunar maria. The edges of the flows are marked by cliffs, or scarps. These appear as wiggly, light lines. Compare with flows on Mars. The large impact crater is Euler Crater, which is 15 miles (23 kilometers) across.

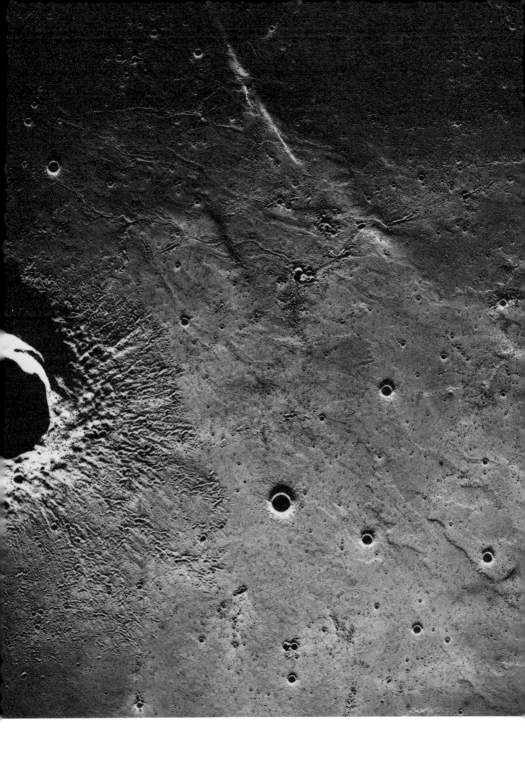

Rilles on the lunar maria. These rilles average about one mile across and although they resemble rivers on Earth, they formed by flowing lava.

They formed when flowing lava created channels on the surface, like rivers of lava. This happens on Earth, too. Rilles may also have formed when lava flowed underground. After the lava had drained away, the roof of the underground channel (called a *lava tube*) collapsed, forming a valley.

The Apollo 15 astronauts guided their spacecraft to a landing next to a rille. Their observations of it, study of the photographs they took, and analyses of the basalts they collected proved that rilles are features formed by volcanic activity.

Domes occur on the Moon. However, instead of forming

masses of lava that plug up a volcano as they do on Earth, lunar domes occur on flat plains on the maria. They form circular, rounded hills up to 10 miles (16 kilometers) across and 2,500 feet (750 meters) high. Some of the larger domes resemble shield volcanoes, but these are rare and not all scientists are convinced that the broad hills are true volcanoes.

Features not seen on Earth that scientists think are related to volcanism are *wrinkle ridges*. These are long, narrow ridges that cross mare plains. Scientists have thought up two ways in which wrinkle ridges may have formed. Both may be right. One idea is that the ridges formed when basalt lava oozed out onto the surface, but did not flow far. The lava piled up, forming a long ridge. The other idea is that a large area of maria was squeezed

Wrinkle ridges on the lunar maria. These look similar to ridges on Mars. The largest impact crater in this picture is about 5 miles (8 kilometers) across.

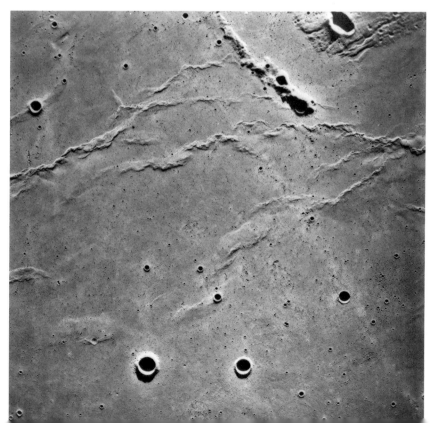

after lava flows had finished erupting. The squeezing may have been caused by the cooling of the Moon—as the Moon or any other body cools it becomes slightly smaller, causing it to wrinkle up, somewhat like a dried apple.

Volcanic cones are present on the Moon, but they are also rare. Where observed, the cones are usually less steep than they are on Earth. The gentler slopes are caused by the lack of air on the Moon. On Earth, when a pyroclastic eruption takes place, many fragments of rock and ash and drops of lava are thrown out of the volcano. Air resistance causes much of the material to fall rapidly to the ground. On the Moon, where there is no air, the fragments travel farther. As a result, a cinder cone on the Moon would be a low, broad hill rather than a built-up cone. Features like these, called *dark-halo craters*, are present in some places on the Moon.

Pictures Are Valuable, but Rock Samples Are Better

As you can see, scientists can learn a lot about a planetary body by peering at photographs of it. However, nothing beats studying an actual chunk of it. Rock samples allow scientists to verify many of the conclusions reached from the study of pictures. A good example of why this is important is the case of the highland volcanic flows.

Before *Apollo 16*, commanded by John Young (who later piloted the first flight of the Space Shuttle), landed in the highlands, many geologists were convinced that the light-colored, smooth plains that are present in many places in the highlands were volcanic deposits. Because the plains were lighter colored than the maria, and because they were somewhat rougher, indi-

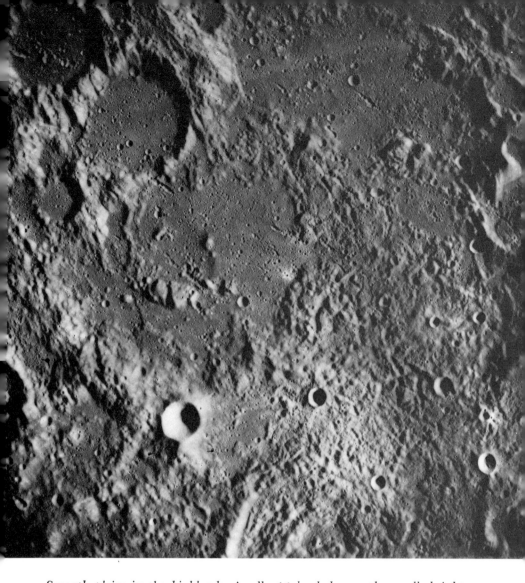

Smooth plains in the highlands. Apollo 16 *landed near the small, bright dot (a young crater) in the center. The astronauts collected rocks that proved that these smooth plains were made by colossal impacts, not by volcanic activity.*

cating a stickier lava, the geologists proposed that the flows were more like andesite than basalt. However, when the rocks were examined back on Earth, scientists discovered that the samples were pieces of meteorite-impact deposits, not volcanic lava flows.

This was an important lesson. The interpretation that smooth plains in the lunar highlands were formed by volcanic eruptions was based on the best available evidence and knowledge. But Nature was trickier than we had thought and had made smooth plains as a by-product of gargantuan meteorite impacts. We must keep this in mind when studying planets from which we have no samples. An old saying tells us that a picture is worth a thousand words. In planetary science, a sample is worth a thousand pictures.

Types of Lunar Volcanic Rock
The first batch of rocks brought back from the Moon proved that the dark plains were composed of basalts. Although the astronauts could not identify lava flows as they walked around on the cratered surface of the airless little planet, the chemical compositions and the shapes of the minerals told scientists that the rocks must have solidified from lava flows. In short, the rocks *look* like volcanic rocks. They contain the same minerals as Earth basalts and the mineral crystals are arranged in patterns typical of Earth basalts. Some rocks contain vesicles; others do not.

Moon basalts are not exactly like Earth basalts, however. The main difference is that they contain no water or other substances that boil at low temperatures. Almost all rocks on Earth contain some water, which usually occurs as part of a mineral (such as mica), not as drops of water. But the Moon rocks contain no water whatsoever. Because Moon basalts formed by melting inside the Moon, the lack of water in the rocks indicates that even the

Apollo 15 astronaut James B. Irwin salutes flag. Hadley Mountain is in the background and Irwin is standing on mare basalt that has been ground up by numerous meteorite impacts. The upsidedown umbrella on the dune buggy (Lunar Roving Vehicle) is an antenna for communication with Earth.

View across a rille (Hadley Rille) at the Apollo 15 *landing site. Thick lava flows form coherent layers. Largest boulders are about 30 feet (9 meters) across.*

inside of the Moon contains no water. This is a basic difference between Earth and the Moon.

Examination of the samples returned by the other Apollo missions and by three unmanned Russian missions confirmed that the dark plains on the Moon are volcanic. The basalts from different parts of the Moon are all different from each other. The

A moon basalt collected by Apollo 17 astronauts Jack Schmitt and Eugene Cernan. The holes, called vesicles, are common in volcanic rocks.

Microscopic view of a Moon basalt. Compare to similar views of Earth and meteorite basalts. Actual area photographed is 8/100 inch (2 millimeters) across.

major difference is in the amount of the element titanium that they contain. Some have as little as 1 percent titanium dioxide, whereas others have as much as 12 percent. Nevertheless, all are basalts and none is andesite.

Although Apollo astronauts did not visit a suspected cinder cone, some samples they collected are like pyroclastic deposits (ash and lava) on Earth. The best example is the "orange soil" collected during the Apollo 17 mission, the last time people traveled to the Moon. The orange soil consists mostly of orange glass. The glass probably erupted from a volcanic vent, perhaps a cinder cone, as tiny droplets of lava that cooled so quickly that they did not have time to form crystals.

Ages of Lunar Volcanic Rocks

Scientists can determine the age of a rock by measuring the amounts of certain radioactive elements present in it. Basalts from the Moon range in age from about 3 billion years up to almost 4 billion years. Although this sounds ancient, maria basalts are the *youngest* rocks returned from the Moon! Rocks from the highlands are even older, a few up to 4½ billion years, the age of the Moon itself.

Although Moon basalts are the youngest of the Moon rocks, they are much older than all but a small percentage of Earth rocks. The oldest rocks on Earth are about 3½ billion years old. The oldest basalts on the ocean floors of Earth are less than 200 million years old. Compared to Earth, the moon's surface is ancient.

Why are Moon rocks so much older than Earth rocks? The answer is simple. Earth is geologically active. Numerous volcanoes erupt each year. Continents drift apart a few inches a year.

(In fact, North America is moving away from Europe at about the same rate your fingernails grow.) Rain, wind, rivers, and floods erode our planet's surface rapidly. But the Moon is simply too little to have kept up such activity. The smaller a planet is, the faster it cools down—and every geologic process is driven by heat. The little Moon cooled down about 3 billion years ago and its geologic engine shut off. The only thing that happens on the Moon now is an occasional meteorite impact that makes a small crater, or even a rarer one that blasts out an impressive hole in the already pockmarked lunar surface. Even less frequently, a spacecraft lands on its barren surface and people hop out to collect rocks and to set up instruments, leaving their footprints behind.

5 Mercury: Old Volcanic Plains

Mercury's Moonlike Surface

Before the *Mariner 10* spacecraft flew past Mercury in 1974, scientists knew little about the planet closest to the sun. Mercury's small size and its close location to the bright sun make viewing difficult from Earth. Even using the most powerful telescope, we cannot see Mercury as well as we can see the Moon with our unaided eyes.

The photographs sent back by the unpiloted *Mariner 10* spacecraft increased our knowledge of Mercury a thousand fold. They revealed an object that looks much like the Moon. Mercury's surface contains heavily cratered areas like the lunar highlands and smooth plains like the lunar maria. Like the Moon, there are thousands of craters, some hundreds of miles across. The largest, the Caloris Basin, is 1,250 miles (2,000 kilometers) across. (Incidentally, except for the Caloris Basin, which means "hot basin," craters on Mercury are named after famous artists, writers, and composers. Thus there are craters with names like Renoir, Tolstoy, and Beethoven.)

The presence of numerous craters demonstrates that Mercury suffered a bombardment just as the Moon did. Earth almost cer-

A close look at Mercury's surface. Most scientists believe that the smooth areas are volcanic.

tainly also experienced a bombardment of huge meteorites, but it is geologically too active to have preserved much of the record. Only by studying other planets do we know that it probably happened.

Smooth Plains—Possible Volcanic Deposits
The main evidence that Mercury's smooth plains are volcanic is that they look like those on the Moon, which scientists know are volcanic. Mercury's plains are as widespread as the moon's

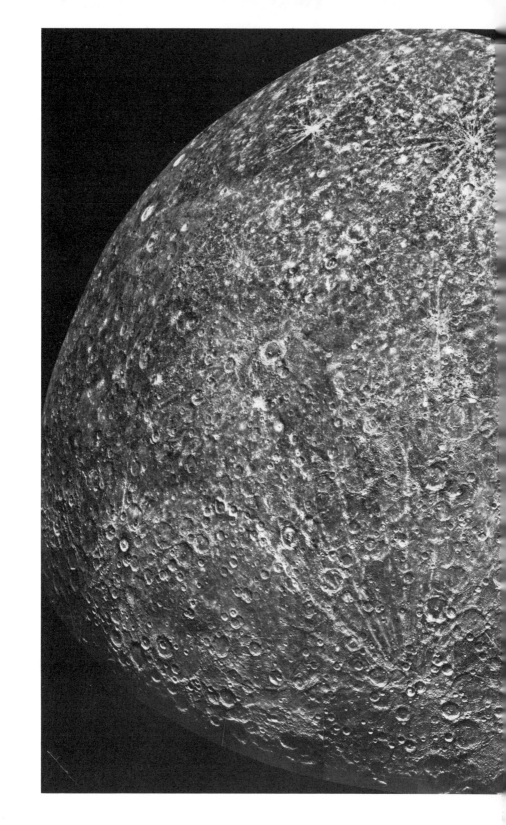

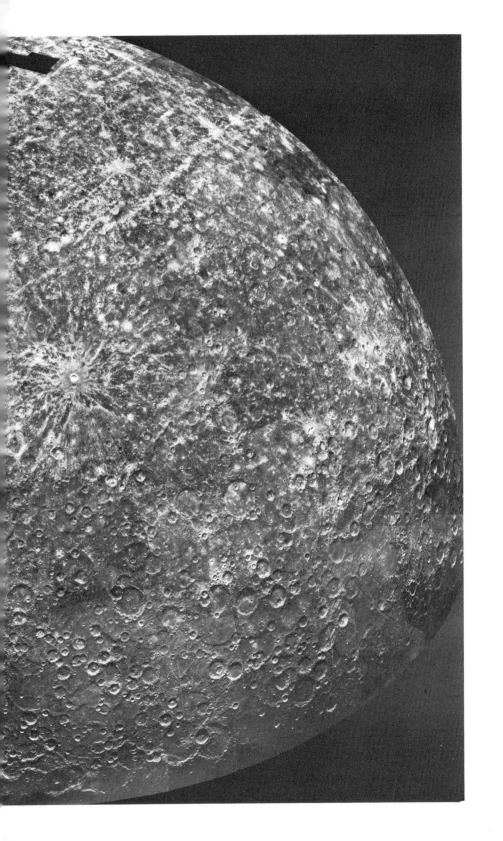

maria and they occur in similar locations within large impact craters. However, except for a few wrinkle ridges, no other volcanic features occur on Mercury. There are no scarps marking the fronts of lava flows, no domes or rilles, and no cinder cones. This obviously makes uncertain the conclusion that the smooth plains on Mercury were formed by lava flows. Nevertheless, most scientists expert in Mercurian geology think the plains are volcanic.

Warning—Plains Can Be Formed by Impacts, Too

Smooth plains in the Moon's highlands were thought to be volcanic until *Apollo 16* returned rocks formed by meteorite impact, not volcanism. This proved that some of the material thrown out of enormous craters flows somewhat like lava does. Consequently, some scientists believe that most, possibly all, of Mercury's plains were formed by impacts.

However, scientists favoring a volcanic origin for Mercury's plains argue that the plains are much more abundant than the impact-deposited plains in the lunar highlands. This suggests that impacts cannot be the only source for the material forming the plains. They also point out that the plains occur in large craters without any indication that the plains' deposits flowed in from the outside, as would be the case with plains made by impact.

It is obvious that we still have a lot to learn about Mercury. We certainly need photographs of the entire planet. (The current set of photographs covers only 54 percent of the surface area.) An automated lander, like those that have landed on Venus and Mars, would give us solid information about the chemical composition of the rocks. This would tell us if the rocks are volcanic and, if so, whether they are basalt or andesite or something else. Best of all, scientists could make some firm conclusions about Mercury's history if automated spacecraft could land, collect some rock samples, then take off and bring the samples back to Earth.

Until we get more information, however, we will have to be content to guess that volcanism took place on Mercury, forming smooth plains much like those on the Moon.

6 Venus: Large Volcanoes— and Maybe Active Ones

Venus, named after the Roman goddess of love and beauty, is a mysterious and inhospitable planet. Its surface is hidden beneath a thick blanket of clouds, making simple photography of it impossible, even from a spacecraft in orbit around it. The *Mariner 10* spacecraft, whipping past on its way to Mercury in 1974, photographed the swirling cloud tops, but could not see the surface below.

The atmosphere on Venus is so dense that the pressure on the surface is ninety times that on the surface of Earth. On our planet, such high pressures are reached 3,000 feet (1 kilometer) below the surface of the ocean. Not only is the air pressure uncomfortably high on Venus, but its temperature is a scalding 860°F (460°C).

All this makes geologic exploration of the planet closest to

The planet Venus, as photographed by the Mariner 10 *spacecraft. Only clouds are visible in this picture, which was taken through an ultraviolet filter. In ordinary light, Venus looks white and featureless.*

Earth extremely difficult. Nevertheless, scientists firmly believe that it is worth the trouble. Venus is an important place to study because it is nearly the same size as Earth. And because size seems to be one of the most important factors in driving the heat engines within planets, scientists wonder if Venus has had volcanoes erupt on its surface, if they are erupting today, and if Venus's crust is broken into moving plates, as is Earth's crust. It is with these questions in mind that scientists have sent a series of spacecraft to Venus.

Peering Through the Clouds
Radar is useful for keeping track of air traffic so airliners do not crash into one another. It is also indispensable in following the development and movement of thunderstorms, some of which spawn dangerous tornadoes. Police find it a great help in catching motorists exceeding the speed limit. Radar is also useful for mapping the surface of cloudy Venus.

The *Pioneer-Venus* orbiter carried a number of instruments when it went into orbit around Venus in 1978. One of the instruments was called a *radar altimeter*, which is a fancy name for a device that uses radar to measure elevations, or topography, on a planetary surface. The radar altimeter sends out a radar signal and measures the time it takes the signal to return. Because radar, which is radio waves, travels at the speed of light, the measuring devices must be very accurate. The longer the time it takes the signal to return, the farther away the ground. As a result, the radar altimeter records mountains as short times, valleys as longer times.

Before *Pioneer-Venus* began mapping Venus's surface, radio

telescopes in Goldstone, California, and Arecibo, Puerto Rico, had bounced radar waves off Venus and obtained some limited information about the planet. *Pioneer-Venus*, however, because it was so much closer to Venus and in an orbit that flew over virtually the entire surface, obtained much more information. It revealed that Venus has a varied and interesting topography, which scientists have divided into *lowlands, rolling plains*, and *highlands*. In keeping with the planet's name, most geologic features on Venus are named after beautiful women of myth and legend. Two prominent lowland areas, for example, are named Atalanta (a swift-footed maiden of Greek legend who offered to marry any man who could beat her in a race) and Guinevere (the wife of King Arthur and good friend of Sir Lancelot).

The lowlands occupy about 27 percent of Venus's surface. Their elevations range from 8,200 feet (2,500 meters) to 1,600 feet (500 meters) below the average radius of the planet. (The radius is the distance from the center of a planet to the surface. Scientists use the average radius as a reference point on Venus the same way we use sea level on Earth. They cannot use sea level on Venus because the planet has no seas or oceans.)

The rolling plains lie between 1,600 feet (500 meters) below the average radius to 4,900 feet (1,500 meters) above the average radius. The plains, which occupy about 65 percent of the surface, contain some long valleys, several plateaus, and some large, circular features that may be impact craters.

The highlands are large, elevated areas that may be akin to continents on Earth. However, in contrast to Earth's continents, which make up 30 percent of our planet's surface, the Venus

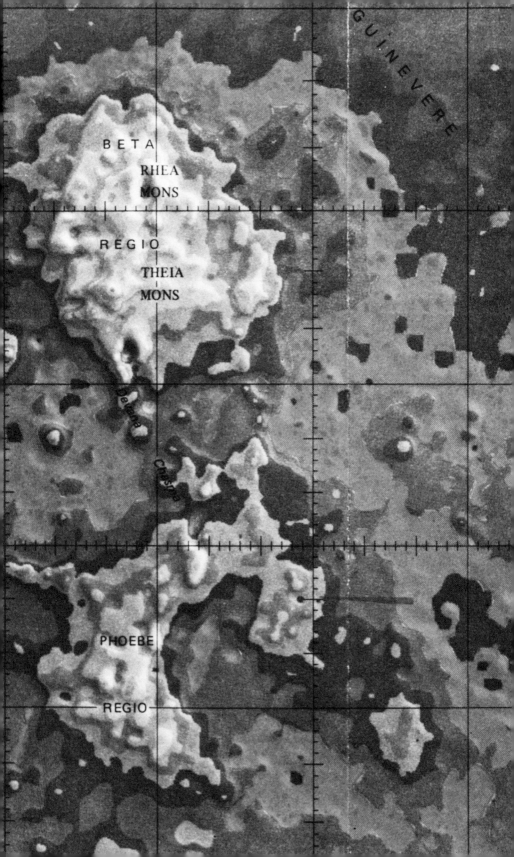

BETA

RHEA
MONS

REGIO

THEIA
MONS

Devana

Chasma

PHOEBE

REGIO

GUINEVERE

highlands occupy only 8 percent of Venus's surface. The high-lands begin at an elevation of about 4,900 feet (1,500 meters) above the average planet radius.

The highlands are concentrated in three main places. The one farthest north is called Ishtar Terra, named after the Babylonian goddess of love. Ishtar Terra is the size of Australia and contains several mountain ranges. The most impressive of these is Maxwell Montes, which rises to a height of 36,000 feet (11,000 meters) above the average Venus radius. It is the highest peak on Venus.

Two highland areas may have large volcanoes. Aphrodite Terra, named for the Greek goddess of love, encompasses an area the size of Africa and is strung out along the Venus equator. The eastern end of Aphrodite Terra contains mountains whose shapes suggest that they are shield volcanoes. Another continental area, Beta Regio, consists of two separate mountains, Theia Mons and Rhea Mons, that also resemble shield volcanoes. Theia Mons is capped by a circular depression that scientists think may be a caldera.

Landing on the Surface
Scientists in the Soviet Union have landed several automated spacecraft on Venus. The first, *Venera 8*, landed in 1974. It was followed the next year by *Venera 9* and *Venera 10*. These space-craft measured the temperature and air pressure on the broiling surface, took air samples to find out what the air is made of

Portion of a map of Venus made by the radar altimeter onboard the Pioneer-Venus *spacecraft. On this computer-generated map, the brightest areas are the highest, the darkest the lowest. The high area called Beta Regio is constructed of two shield volcanoes.*

ВЕНЕРА-14   ОБРАБОТКА ИППИ АН СССР И ЦДКС

ВЕНЕРА-14   ОБРАБОТКА ИППИ АН СССР И ЦДКС

This panorama of the surface of Venus was obtained by the Venera 14 *spacecraft, which landed in March, 1982. The relatively smooth landscape may be lava flows or pyroclastic (ash and lava) deposits.*

(mostly carbon dioxide, no oxygen or water vapor), and did some chemical analyses of the ground. The results suggested that the rocks at two of the landing sites could be basalt. The rocks at the other site might be granite.

These automated spacecraft measured only a few elements, so the conclusions about rock composition were uncertain. This uncertainty was erased when *Venera 13* and *Venera 14* landed near Beta Regio, one of the suspected volcanic areas, in March, 1982. These spacecraft carried elaborate equipment to measure rock and soil compositions. The results, which were reported at the Thirteenth Lunar and Planetary Science Conference in Houston, Texas, less than two weeks after landing, proved that Beta

Regio is composed of basalt. The rocks are not unlike Earth basalt. Apparently numerous lava flows erupted from the interior of Venus and flowed onto its surface, forming large shield volcanoes.

The unpiloted Russian spacecraft also took pictures of the areas on which they landed. The photographs show a stark, smooth terrain. Some scientists believe that the smoothest areas may be pyroclastic deposits, not simply lava flows, which are usually rougher in appearance.

Active Volcanoes?

Many scientists believe that the large volcanoes on Venus are also active, spewing out lava right now. The *Pioneer-Venus* spacecraft detected an extra pull of gravity as it passed over one of the suspected volcanoes. Because the strength of the force of gravity depends on the *mass* of rock doing the pulling, the excess gravity associated with volcanoes on Venus indicates that the volcanoes must be in the process of being built. Otherwise, there would be no excess gravity.

Scientists are also intrigued by lightning in Venus's atmosphere, which seems to be concentrated above the volcanic features of Beta Regio and the eastern end of Aphrodite Terra. Lightning also occurs during volcanic eruptions on Earth, so perhaps some volcanoes on Venus are squirting lava out right at this moment. If so, the tops of Venus's shield volcanoes must be terrifying places: red hot lava bursts forth, lightning bolts zigzag across the sky, the air is a sizzling 860°F, and the air pressure squeezes intensely at ninety times that on Earth.

Questions

Venus certainly has had lava erupt onto its surface. In at least two places, the lava seems to have been similar to Earth basalt. Scientists are not positive, however, that Venus has active volcanoes. Nor are they sure if plate tectonics operates on Venus. Some scientists believe that large plates do not grind past one another on Venus as they do on Earth, but other scientists suggest that the information obtained by the *Pioneer-Venus* spacecraft is not sufficient to allow a conclusion to be reached about whether plate tectonics helps shape the Venus landscape or not.

All scientists agree, however, that we need to learn more about Venus. The next American mission to Venus will probably be another radar mapper. This one will be much better than the one carried by *Pioneer-Venus* and will be capable of determining whether continents drift about on Venus's surface and whether volcanoes are erupting today.

Scientists have peered through the thick clouds surrounding Venus, but they are not satisfied. The glimpses have only made them more curious.

7 Mars: The Largest Volcanoes in the Solar System

Enormous shield volcanoes rise from the reddish surface of the planet Mars. These volcanoes are the most impressive of an array of interesting geologic features on the fourth planet from the sun.

The Red Planet, as Mars is sometimes called because of its red color (which is caused by the presence of iron oxide), is the best explored planet other than Earth and our Moon. Although not quite the pleasant place depicted in Ray Bradbury's science fiction book *The Martian Chronicles*, it is certainly an interesting world. Mars is much cooler than Earth. Even at noon on a summer's day at the equator, the temperature is rarely above the freezing point of water (32°F, 0°C). The polar regions are so nippy that much of the ice is frozen carbon dioxide (also called "dry ice"), which forms on Mars at temperatures less than 189°F (123°C) *below* zero. The air is made mostly of carbon dioxide, contains almost no oxygen, and is only 1/150 as thick as Earth's atmosphere. The low air pressure is similar to the pressure on Earth at an altitude of 120,000 feet (37 kilometers).

Mars has been explored by several unpiloted spacecraft. Some

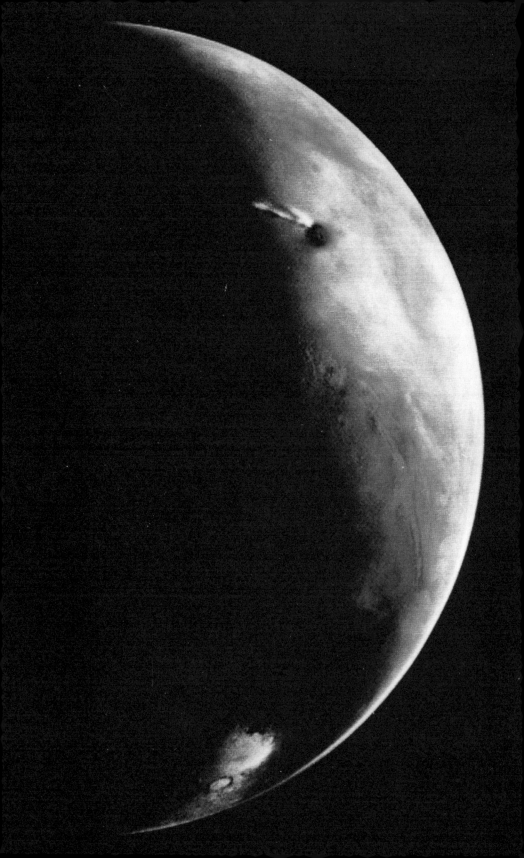

orbited the planet, sent pictures of the surface back to Earth, and made other measurements. Two Viking spacecraft landed successfully on Mars's barren surface. The landers took pictures on the ground and conducted a number of scientific experiments designed to determine if life exists on Mars. Although no signs of life were found, scientists were delighted to learn about the geology and volcanic history of Mars.

The View from Orbit
Mars is like Earth's Moon in many ways. About half the surface consists of heavily cratered terrain that resembles the moon's highlands. Like the Moon, Mars contains some enormous circular basins that were formed by the impact of immense meteorites. The largest basin, Hellas, is 1,000 miles (1,600 kilometers) across. Mars also has smooth plains, many of which seem to be volcanic.

On the other hand, Mars is unlike the Moon is many other ways. Several obvious volcanoes dot its surface. Large canyons formed by the martian crust cracking in places and then eroding (possibly by water flowing in torrential floods) occur on Mars, but not on the Moon. One canyon, called Valles Marineris, stretches across Mars for about 3,000 miles (4,800 kilometers), the distance of New York to Los Angeles. The canyon is up to 300 miles (500 kilometers) wide, and is four times deeper than the Grand Canyon in Arizona. Finally, although Mars's atmosphere is thin compared to Earth's, it is still thick enough to blow dust and sand around. Consequently, dust storms occur on Mars and large fields

The planet Mars has craters, lava plains, and enormous volcanoes.

Olympus Mons, the largest volcano in the solar system, is a shield volcano. It measures 430 miles (700 kilometers) across at its base and the caldera at its summit is 50 miles (80 kilometers) across. It rises 65,000 feet (20 kilometers) above the surrounding plains.

of dunes form. The Moon, of course, is totally airless, so there can be no wind.

The most startling geologic features on Mars are the shield volcanoes. Even to geologists who have worked on large Earth volcanoes, the Martian ones are astounding. The largest, Olympus Mons, is 430 miles (700 kilometers) across at its base and rises to a height of 65,000 feet (20 kilometers) above the surrounding plains. Because the plains themselves are elevated, Olympus Mons rises 88,000 feet (27 kilometers) above the average Mars radius.

Ascraeus Mons is another large shield volcano on Mars. It is about 250 miles (400 kilometers) across.

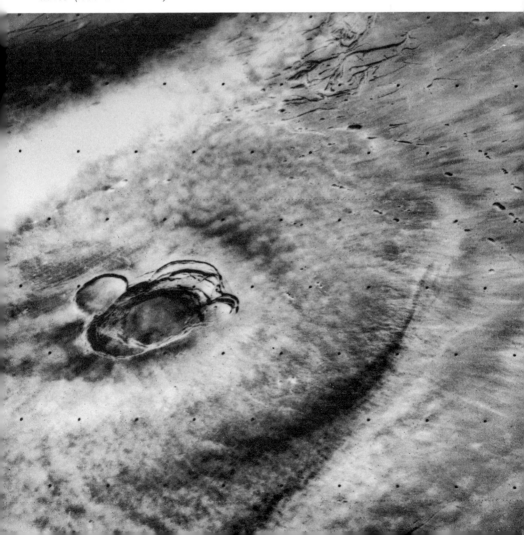

Lava flows on Mars. The edges of each flow are marked by cliffs (the wiggly lines) just as they are on Earth and the Moon. One lava flow has poured into the large impact crater on the right; this crater is 19 miles (30 kilometers) across.

A caldera 50 miles (80 kilometers) across adorns the top of Olympus Mons.

All of the volcanic mountains on Mars have gently sloping sides. Because similar volcanoes on Earth are made of basalt, which flows easily, scientists believe those on Mars are also built of basalt. Based on the number of meteorite impact craters on Martian shield volcanoes, which allows scientists to estimate the time since lavas stopped erupting, it appears that the volcanoes shut off about 200 million years ago. None is active today.

Mars contains large areas of smooth plains. Many of these are clearly volcanic like the moon's maria. Some of the plains fill large basins, such as the Hellas basin, just as the lunar maria do. The evidence that the plains were formed by lava eruptions includes the presence of flow fronts marking the places where individual lava flows stopped moving, wrinkle ridges, cinder cones, and small shield volcanoes. However, some plains areas do not have some or all of these features. In these cases, the plains may have formed by meteorite impact, like the plains in the moon's highlands.

Ridges on these lava plains on Mars look much like those on the Moon.

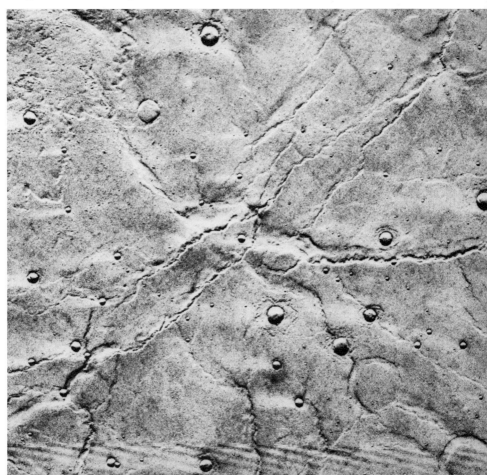

Close-up of the surface of Mars, taken by Viking Lander 2. *The boulders contain vesicles, a common feature of volcanic rocks. The*

The View from the Ground

In July and September, 1976, two automated spacecraft landed on smooth, volcanic plains on Mars. Called *Viking Landers 1* and *2*, they carried cameras and devices designed to detect life, measure the chemical composition of the soil, determine the composition of the Martian air, and measure the strength of the planet's magnetic field.

Panorama of the martian surface. Boulders litter the landscape all the way

largest boulders are about 8 inches (20 centimeters) across. The circular object in the lower right is one of the landing pads of the spacecraft.

The first photographs sent back by *Viking Lander 1*, the first to land, revealed a barren landscape. A boulder 6 feet (2 meters) across lay only 30 feet (10 meters) from the lander; hitting it during landing would have caused the spacecraft to tip over. On the horizon, the electronic eyes of the spacecraft could make out the faint outline of a meteorite impact crater.

to the horizon.

The Viking landers confirmed the presence of volcanic rock in two ways. First, some of the rocks visible in the photographs taken by *Viking Lander 2* contain vesicles, frozen gas bubbles commonly present in volcanic rocks. Second, the instrument that measured the chemical makeup of the Martian soil indicated that basalts (not andesites) are present, though the soil itself seems to be made mostly of clay. Clay forms on Earth when water flows over bare rock. Scientists do not think, however, that liquid water exists on Mars today, though ice may exist beneath the surface. Some believe that the clay may have formed when the lavas erupted through layers of frozen water beneath the Martian surface. The flat tops of some volcanoes on Mars support this idea because on Earth flat-top volcanoes form when lava erupts beneath ice in places like Iceland.

Basalt lava certainly erupted onto Mars's surface and it formed huge shield volcanoes and broad plains. However, scientists are not certain of exactly when the volcanism took place or if it may happen again. They also do not know the precise chemical composition of the lavas, which limits how much they can say about the inside of the planet. Most scientists agree that the next logical step in the study of Mars is to send an automated spacecraft to return some samples of rock and soil. It will be an exciting day when it happens!

8 Asteroids and Meteorites: The Oldest Lava Flows

The Meteorite-Asteroid Connection

When trying to figure out the geologic history of a planet, nothing helps more than having actual rock samples from it. Our understanding of Earth's moon would be far less complete if Apollo astronauts had not collected rock samples or if Russian unmanned spacecraft had not returned samples of soil. We would know much more about Mercury, Venus, and Mars if we had even one sample from each planet. In this regard, asteroid exploration is a real bargain: gravitational forces and collisions in the asteroid belt deliver chunks of asteroids to us free of charge. These chunks are called *meteorites.*

How do scientists know that meteorites came from asteroids? There are several reasons. The first is that before meteorites hit Earth, they traveled in orbits that extend to the asteroid belt. Scientists determine these orbits by photographing *meteors* as they blaze through Earth's atmosphere. (If a meteor is observed landing on Earth, the rock collected is called a meteorite.)

The second reason is that the histories of many types of meteor-

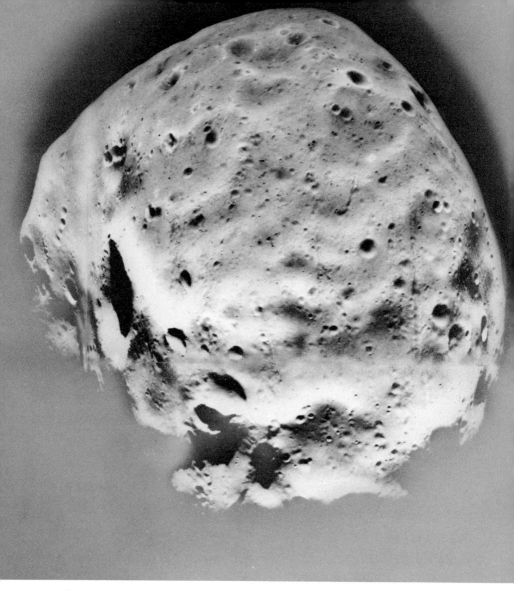

Asteroids probably look like Phobos, a moon of Mars (although Phobos is not volcanic). Phobos is cratered and has a lumpy shape, measuring 17 by 12 miles (27 by 19 kilometers).

ites indicate that they must have originated on small bodies, not on large planets.

Finally, we know meteorites come from asteroids because the

way they reflect light is the same way that asteroids reflect light. Even the most powerful telescope is not potent enough to see any surface features on an asteroid, but by using a method called *reflectance spectrophotometry* astronomers can determine what types of minerals are present on the surface of an asteroid. The results of measurements of the 150 largest asteroids indicate that they reflect light the same way as the known types of meteorites. Hence, they are made of the same minerals.

Astronomers do not know what asteroids actually look like, but they have a fairly good idea. Asteroids are probably heavily cratered, lumpy, irregularly shaped objects. They probably look like the moons of Mars, which most scientists think are asteroids captured by Mars's gravity.

Many Types of Meteorites

There are over 3,500 individual meteorites in the world's collections. Some meteorites break up in the atmosphere and, consequently, are represented by thousands of individual specimens. Many meteorites have been observed to fall, but most have been found by observant people. Also, since 1976 there has been a concerted effort to collect meteorites in the frozen wastelands of Antarctica. Ironically, Antarctica is so difficult to work in because of the extreme cold that the preparations that the collecting teams must make are almost as complicated as a trip to another planet.

Scientists recognize three main types of meteorites: *Irons* are remarkable rocks (if you can call them rocks) composed almost entirely of metallic iron-nickel. *Stones* are rocky meteorites of various types. *Stony-irons*, as the name implies, are about half metallic iron and half rock.

77

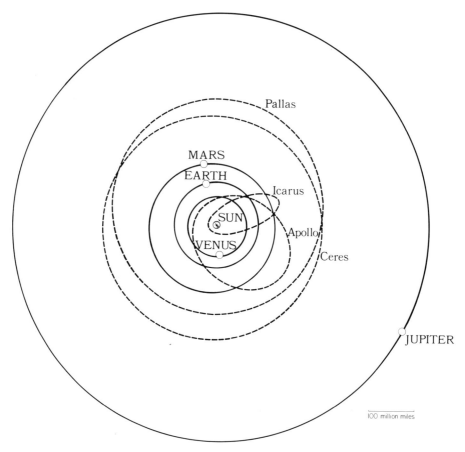

Orbits of a few asteroids are shown by dashed lines on this diagram. Some asteroids, such as Icarus and Apollo, pass fairly close to the sun and cross Earth's orbit. Meteorites follow similar paths, so are probably pieces of asteroids. Other asteroids are confined to the asteroid belt between Mars and Jupiter.

Stone meteorites are the most abundant. There are two main types. One type, the *chondrites*, are rocks that contain bits and pieces of material left over from the time the planets were forming. They are fascinating objects that may hold the key to our understanding of planet formation. The other type of stone meteorite, the *achondrites*, formed by melting inside one or more asteroids. The achondrites are volcanic rocks, most of them basalts.

Volcanic Meteorites

The most common achondrites are the *basaltic achondrites*. These meteorites have chemical compositions somewhat like Earth basalts, but they are more like Moon basalts, especially in their total lack of water. The basaltic achondrites have mineral shapes like basalts from Earth and Moon. One even has vesicles.

The basaltic achondrites are 4½ billion years old. This is the age of the solar system itself. Consequently, the asteroid or asteroids on which these basalt lavas erupted must have heated up rapidly after forming. If such little planets like asteroids heated

Microscopic photograph of a meteorite basalt. Note how similar it looks to Earth and Moon basalts. The actual area photographed is 8/100 inch (2 millimeters).

up so fast, scientists believe that large planets probably heated up as well. Planets, therefore, must have formed hot, so volcanoes may have started erupting onto Earth's surface from the time our planet formed.

Telescopic observations of the asteroids indicate that one asteroid in particular may be the source for the basaltic achondrites. The way in which it reflects light matches the way basaltic achondrites reflect light, so the asteroid may be covered with rock much like basalt. This asteroid is Vesta, the third largest. It is 341 miles (549 kilometers) across. Perhaps someday a spacecraft will speed past Vesta and observe the presence of lava flows or perhaps even little volcanoes.

Meteorites from Mars?

The basaltic achondrites are the most abundant volcanic meteorites, but there is another interesting group. Nicknamed the SNC meteorites (pronounced "snick"), only nine of them are known. They are of special interest because they formed only about 1 billion years ago. Because scientists think that small bodies the size of asteroids cool too fast to still be partly molten inside as recently as a billion years ago, they surmise that the SNC meteorites come from a larger planet.

The best bet for the larger planet is Mars. The moon is out of the running because the youngest basalts there are 3 billion years old, not 1 billion. We know Mars has volcanoes on its surface and that many of them are probably even less than a billion years old.

The problem is, how did the SNC meteorites leave Mars? Volcanic eruptions are not powerful enough. Some scientists suggest that a meteorite impact may have blasted some rocks off the planet's surface. They point out that if there is frozen water beneath the ground on Mars it would boil rapidly during an impact and give a boost to the rocks flying out of a growing crater. Other scientists doubt the added boost would be enough and still others believe that any rock romoved from Mars would be melted in the process.

The idea that some meteorites come from Mars is unproven, but certainly exciting. We may already have chunks of the planet Mars in our laboratories on Earth!

Io, a moon of Jupiter, is the most volcanically active body in the solar system. In color, its surface is dominated by orange and yellow. These vivid colors are caused by the presence of large amounts of sulfur and sulfur dioxide. Io is about the size of Earth's moon.

9   Io: Many Active Volcanoes

Jupiter is the largest planet in the solar system. A giant red spot larger than Earth swirls in its dynamic atmosphere. The red spot and other smaller blobs of gases are powerful storms raging in Jupiter's colorful atmosphere. However, for all its size and its turbulent air, Jupiter has no volcanoes.

The giant planet does have fifteen moons circling it. Four of them are much larger than the others and were discovered in 1610 by Galileo. To honor this brilliant Italian scientist, these four are called the *Galilean satellites*. In order of increasing distance from Jupiter, the Galilean satellites are Io, Europa, Ganymede, and Callisto. All are about the size of Earth's moon, but Ganymede and Callisto are half rock and half ice. Io and Europa are made mostly of rock materials. They are all interesting, but Io is the featured attraction.

Active Volcanoes on Io
When the *Voyager 1* spacecraft passed Jupiter in March, 1979, it sent back thousands of pictures of Jupiter and its satellites. The photographs of Io (pronounced either "eye-oh" or "ee-oh") contained some surprises. Eight volcanoes were erupting vigorously

and spewing lava onto Io's orange surface. When *Voyager 2* reached the area four months later, six of the volcanoes were still active and another had appeared. Io is obviously the most volcanically active body in the solar system.

The vivid color of Io's surface is caused by the presence of vast amounts of sulfur and sulfur dioxide. These are unusual substances, but even Earth volcanoes contain some. Most of the lava on Io, however, seems to be molten sulfur, not molten rock. Scientists are not sure how much basalt or similar lava is being erupted on Io.

Io not only has numerous active volcanoes, but the volcanoes erupt with terrific force. They jet out material at speeds of up to 2,200 miles per hour (3,600 kilometers per hour). This is much faster than even the most awesome Earth volcano.

Dark lava flows dribble down the slopes of a volcano on Io. Smooth areas are probably deposits of sulfur compounds.

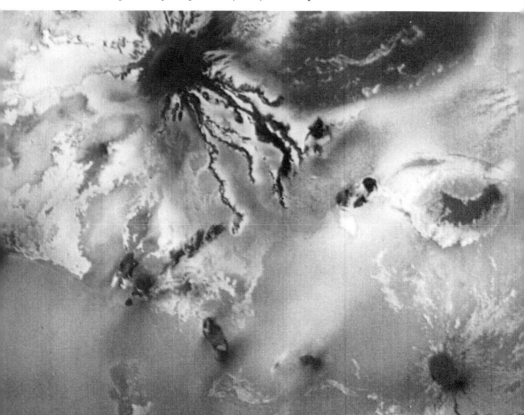

Scientists have observed several volcanic features on Io, in addition to active volcanoes. There are shield volcanoes with calderas decorating their tops. Individual lava flows can be seen dribbling down the slopes of the volcanoes. In some places, lava seems to have erupted through fissures rather than from a volcano.

An Unusual Source of Heat

In most cases, the heat needed to run a planet's volcano machine comes from the decay of radioactive elements. (When a radioactive element decays to another element, some heat is released.) Just as a cup of soup cools faster than a potful, a small planet cools faster than a larger one. This causes small planets to become volcanically inactive sooner than larger ones. As a result, the smallest planets have the oldest volcanoes: asteroid basalts are 4½ billion years old. Basalts from the moon, which is larger than any asteroid, are 3 billion years old; those on Mars, a medium-sized inner planet, may be as young as 200 million years; and Earth and Venus are still volcanically active. But Io, the size of Earth's moon, is still piping hot. Clearly some other factor must be involved.

The other factor stems from Io's location close to the solar system's largest planet. Jupiter heats Io. Io has a somewhat wobbly orbit that causes it to move closer and farther from Jupiter. Jupiter's gravity pulls on Io while Europa and Ganymede's gravity pull from the other direction. All these gravitational tugs combine with the wobbly orbit to raise tides on Io, causing its solid surface to bulge up and down 300 feet (100 meters). This movement pulls and pushes Io's insides, raising the temperature and causing melting and volcanism.

10 Searching for More Volcanoes

The space age has turned specks of light in the night sky into panoramic views of other worlds. We have learned an incredible amount about other planets and the volcanoes on them. Yet we still have much to learn.

Are the smooth plains on Mercury volcanic? Or did they form when enormous meteorites blasted out gigantic craters?

Are the large, shieldlike mountains on Venus really volcanoes that were constructed by the eruption of numerous basalt lava flows? If they are volcanoes, are they active today? Does plate tectonics operate on Venus as it does on Earth?

How old are the volcanoes on Mars? Are they made of basalt, or do other types of volcanic rocks also occur on the Red Planet? Do the billion-year-old SNC meteorites come from Mars?

What do asteroids look like up close? Do they resemble the moons of Mars, as most scientists believe? How did lava erupt on them? Are there little volcanic mountains on these small planets?

Io is spewing lava from its insides at a faster rate than any other body we know about, but are the lavas all sulfur? Or do basalts or andesites also erupt on Io?

Saturn's large satellite, Titan, is hidden by a thick atmosphere.

The first reusable spacecraft, the Space Shuttle Columbia, *blasts off from the Kennedy Space Center in Florida on April 12, 1981.*

What's going on beneath this gaseous shroud? Are volcanoes erupting? Did they ever erupt?

What are the moons of Uranus and Neptune like? Are volcanoes squirting lava from their insides?

Did little Pluto ever erupt lavas onto its frigid surface? Do vast plains of basalt or other volcanic rock fill ancient impact scars as they do on Earth's moon?

Planetary scientists obviously have their work cut out for them. Much of the United States's effort in space exploration will involve an entirely new type of spacecraft that will use the Space Shuttle as the launch vehicle. The Shuttle, the first reusable spacecraft, blasted off for the first time at 7:00 A.M. on April 12, 1981, from the Kennedy Space Center in Cape Canaveral, Florida. This first test-flight ended successfully 54 hours, 21 minutes, and 52 seconds after launch when astronaut John Young guided the ninety-nine-ton spacecraft-airplane to a landing at Edwards Air Force Base, California. It was Young's fifth flight, including two to the Moon (one landing on it), making him the most experienced space pilot.

Planetary scientists hope the Shuttle will eventually carry unmanned spacecraft into orbit around Earth and then launch the automated explorers on flights to the far reaches of the solar system. They also hope the Shuttle will be used to help establish permanent research laboratories in space, including research stations on the Moon. From a base on the Moon, the geologic exploration of Earth's neighbor will begin in earnest, as will use of the Moon's resources.

The United States will not be alone in exploring the solar system. The Soviet Union will continue its vigorous program of space exploration, including more trips to the hostile surface of Venus. Soviet scientists also plan a joint venture with France to study Halley's comet, which in 1986 makes one of its infrequent appearances in our part of the solar system. Other European nations will join forces with Japan to send spacecraft to this fascinating visitor from the outermost solar system.

Perhaps one day all planetary missions will be done cooperatively by scientists from all nations on Earth. After all, we all share the same planet and we all wonder how it formed and how its volcanoes work. To find out how volcanoes work we must study them *everywhere* they occur.

Glossary

ACHONDRITE—A type of stone meteorite formed by melting inside an asteroid. Most are volcanic rocks.

ANDESITE—One of the two major types of volcanic rocks that occur on Earth. Andesites contain more silicon dioxide (56 to 65 percent) than do basalts and occur mostly in composite volcanoes. None has been discovered on another planet.

ASTEROIDS—The small bodies that revolve around the sun between the orbits of Mars and Jupiter.

BASALT—One of the two most abundant types of volcanic rock types on Earth. Basalts contain less silicon dioxide (less than 55 percent) than do andesites and form shield volcanoes on Earth, Venus, and Mars, and vast lava plains on Earth, the Moon, Venus, Mars, and some asteroids.

BASALTIC ACHONDRITES—Meteorites formed when basalt lava erupted onto the surface of an asteroid.

CALDERA—A large (several miles across), circular depression formed by the collapse of a volcano.

CHONDRITES—Stony meteorites distinguished by the presence of millimeter-sized particles called "chondrules." Chondrites have not been melted.

CINDER CONE—A cone-shaped hill or small mountain, rarely higher than 300 feet (500 meters), built mostly of pyroclastic materials.

CLAY—Finely crystalline, water-bearing minerals formed from other minerals by chemical reactions with water.

COMETS—Icy objects located far beyond the orbits of the planets.

COMPOSITE VOLCANO—A cone-shaped volcanic mountain formed mainly by eruptions of andesite lava and pyroclastic material.

CORE—The central region of a planet, frequently made of different materials than the surrounding regions (mantle and crust). Earth's core is composed of iron and nickel.

CRATER—A circular, bowl-shaped depression. Craters can form on top of volcanoes (in which case they are smaller than calderas) or by the impact of giant meteorites.

CRUST—The outermost, and smallest, zone of Earth. The mantle is beneath the crust. Other planets also have crusts.

CRYSTALS—A solid with an orderly internal arrangement of atoms. All minerals are crystals.

CRYSTALLIZE—To form a crystal from a noncrystalline substance such as a lava.

DARK HALO CRATER—A crater on the Moon surrounded by a low, broad, dark hill thought to be formed by the eruption of pyroclastic material from a small volcanic vent.

DOME—A mass of lava with steep sides that frequently plugs up a volcano.

FISSURE—A long crack in a planet's surface from which lava erupts.

FLOOD BASALTS—Basalts that erupted from fissures and formed large plateaus and plains.

GABBRO—A coarse-grained rock with similar minerals and chemical composition as basalts, but which formed at depth in Earth.

GALILEAN SATELLITES—The four largest moons (or satellites) of Jupiter, which were discovered by Galileo. In order of increasing distance from Jupiter, they are Io, Europa, Ganymede, and Callisto.

GLASS—A solid material that does not have the ordered internal arrangement of atoms characteristic of crystals.

GRANITE—An intrusive rock type having more silicon dioxide than andesite or granodiorite.

GRANODIORITE—A coarse-grained type of rock formed when magma of andesite composition solidifies at depth in Earth.

GRAVITY—A force in which the mass of one object attracts the mass of another.

IMPACT CRATER—A circular depression made when a meteorite smashes into a planetary surface at a high velocity. Impact craters are much larger than the impacting meteorite.

INTRUSIVE—A term used to describe rocks that crystallized at depth in a planet.

IRON METEORITES—A meteorite made almost entirely of metallic iron and nickel.

LAVA—Molten rock that has reached the surface of a planet. Before it reaches the surface, molten rock is called "magma."

MAGMA—Molten rock beneath the surface of a planet. Once it reaches the surface, magma is called "lava."

MAGMA CHAMBER—An immense pool of magma below a planet's surface. Magma chambers supply volcanoes with magma.

MANTLE—The major zone of Earth located between the crust and the core. Other inner planets probably have mantles underlying their crusts.

MARIA—Relatively smooth, dark-colored areas on Earth's moon that are covered with lava flows. Similar features exist on some other planets.

MASS—The amount of matter in an object. A bag of rocks is heavier than a bag of feathers because it has more mass.

METEOR—The flash of light seen when an object, such as a meteorite or a fragment of a comet, enters Earth's atmosphere at a high velocity.

METEORITE—Stony or metallic body that has fallen to Earth from space.

MID-OCEAN RIDGE—An undersea mountain chain formed by the eruption of basalt lava at places where two plates spread apart.

MINERAL—A naturally occurring solid material that has a definite chemical composition and internal arrangement of atoms.

MOON—A natural body that orbits (revolves around) a planet, also called "natural satellites."

ORBIT—The circular path a planet follows around the sun or a moon follows around a planet.

PHENOCRYST—A crystal much larger than those surrounding it.

PLANET—Rocky or gaseous bodies that orbit the sun.

PLATEAU BASALTS—Another term for "flood basalts."

PLATE TECTONICS—The theory that Earth's crust and uppermost mantle are divided into huge blocks (plates) that move, and the relationship of these movements to volcanism, earthquakes, and mountain building.

PUMICE—A volcanic rock filled with numerous trapped gas bubbles, which give it a frothy appearance. The trapped bubbles make pumice so lightweight that some pieces can float on water.

PYROCLASTIC DEPOSITS—Rock fragments and drops of lava thrown out of a volcanic vent.

RADAR—A type of electromagnetic radiation with much higher frequencies than visible light.

RADAR ALTIMETER—A device which uses radar signals to measure elevations on a planetary surface.

RILLES—Long, curved or straight valleys on the lunar maria. Similar features also occur on Mars and possibly on Mercury.

SATELLITE—Any body that orbits another. Moons are natural satellites.

SCARP—A cliff or other steep slope.

SHIELD VOLCANO—A broad volcano with gently sloping sides formed by the eruption of basalt lava.

SNC METEORITES—A group of meteorites with relatively young ages (slightly over one billion years) that may have come from Mars.

SOLAR SYSTEM—The sun and all the objects (planets, moons, asteroids, and comets) that orbit it.

SOLIDIFICATION—The process by which a liquid (including molten rock) becomes a solid.

STAR—A large, gaseous body undergoing nuclear fusion in its interior and emitting light and other energy. The sun is a star.

STONE METEORITE—A meteorite composed chiefly of rock.

STONY-IRON METEORITE—A meteorite composed of approximately half rock and half metallic iron.

SUN—The star residing at the center of our solar system and around which all the other objects revolve.

VENT—An opening in a planet's crust through which lava, pyroclastic materials, or gases erupt.

VESICLES—Gas bubbles trapped in a lava as the lava solidifies.

VOLCANO—A cone-shaped mountain or hill built by the eruption of lava or pyroclastic materials.

WRINKLE RIDGES—Ridges found on the surfaces of lunar maria and marialike areas on Mars and Mercury.

Index

Achondrite, 79, 90
  basaltic, 79–80, 90
Aconcagua, Mount (Argentina), 28
Altimeter, radar, 58, 61, 64, 92
American Plate, 33
Andesite, 21–23, 24, 26, 28, 32, 33, 34, 38, 43, 48, 86, 90
Aphrodite Terra (Venus), 61, 63
Apollo (asteroid), 78
Apollo 15 mission, 40, 45, 46
Apollo 16 mission, 42, 43, 54
Apollo 17 mission, 47, 48
Ascraeus Mons (Mars), 69
Asteroids, 10, 12, 13, 18, 19, 75–80, 86, 90
Atalanta (Venus), 59

Basalt, 21–23, 28, 30, 32, 33, 34, 38, 40, 41, 44, 45, 46, 47, 48, 63, 64, 70, 74, 79, 84, 85, 86, 88, 90
  flood, 28, 30, 33, 38, 91
  plateau, 28, 92
Basaltic achondrites, 79–80, 90
Beta Regio (Venus), 61, 62–63
Bradbury, Ray, 65

Calderas, 24, 25, 37, 38, 61, 68, 70, 85, 90
Callisto (moon of Jupiter), 83
Caloris Basin (Mercury), 50
Cascade Mountains, 9, 26
Ceres (asteroid), 18
Cernan, Eugene, 47
Chondrites, 78, 90
Cinder cones, 26, 41, 71, 90
Circum-Pacific belt, 30

Clay, 74, 90
Columbia (Space Shuttle), 87, 88
Comets, 18–19, 89, 90
Composite volcanoes, 26–28, 30, 38, 90
Continental drift, 30, 33, 48, 64
Core, defined, 90
Craters, 24, 37–38, 41, 50, 54, 67, 70, 73, 90
  dark-halo, 42, 91
  impact, 91
Crust, defined, 90
Crystallize, defined, 90
Crystals, defined, 90

Dark-halo craters, 42, 91
Domes, 28, 40–41, 91

Earth (planet), 9–12, 13, 15, 16, 18, 19, 20, 21–34, 48, 50–51
Earthquakes, 30
Emi Koussi (Africa), 25
Euler Crater (Earth's Moon), 38
Europa (moon of Jupiter), 17, 83, 85

Feldspar, 22
Fissures, 28, 85, 91
Flood basalts, 28, 30, 33, 38, 91
Fujiyama, Mount (Japan), 27

Gabbro, 34, 91
Galilean satellites, 83, 91
Galileo, 37, 83
Ganymede (moon of Jupiter), 83, 85
Glass, defined, 91
Granite, 34, 62, 91
Granodiorite, 34, 91

Gravity, defined, 91
Guinevere (Venus), 59

Hadley Mountain (Earth's Moon), 45
Hadley Rille (Earth's Moon), 46
Halley's comet, 19, 89
Hawaii, 24, 30
Hellas (Mars), 67, 71

Icarus (asteroid), 78
Intrusive rocks, 34, 91
Io (moon of Jupiter), 10, 12, 17, 18,
  82, 83–85, 86
Irwin, James B., 45
Ishtar Terra (Venus), 61

Jupiter (planet), 10, 13, 14, 16, 17, 18,
  83–85
  Moons of. *See* Callisto, Europa,
    Ganymede, Io
  Red Spot, 17, 83

Kennedy Space Center, 10, 88

Lava, 21–24, 26, 28, 29, 30, 32, 33–34,
  36, 37, 38, 40, 41, 46, 63, 64, 70, 71,
  74, 79, 84, 86, 88, 91
Lava tube, 40
Lightning, volcanoes and, 63

Magma, 34, 37, 91
Magma chamber, 23, 91
Mantle, defined, 91
Mare Imbrium (Earth's Moon), 38
Maria (Earth's Moon), 37, 38, 39, 41,
  91
Mariner 10 spacecraft, 50, 57
Mars (planet), 10, 12, 15, 18, 55, 65–
  74, 80–81, 86
Martian Chronicles, The, (Bradbury),
  65
Mass, defined, 91
Mauna Kea (Hawaii), 24
Mauna Loa (Hawaii), 24
Maxwell Montes (Venus), 61

Mercury (planet), 10, 12, 15, 18, 50–
  55, 86
Meteorites, 75–81, 91
  SNC, 80, 86, 92
  stone, 77, 92
  stony-iron, 77, 92
  types of, 77–81
  volcanic, 79–80
Meteors, 75, 91
Mid-ocean ridge, 28, 91
Mineral, defined, 91
Moon(s), 13, 17–18, 19
  defined, 92
  Earth's, 10, 19, 35–49, 75, 88
  Jupiter's, 10, 12, 17, 18, 82, 83–85, 86

Neptune (planet), 12, 17, 18, 88
Nuclear fusion, 15

Olympus Mons (Mars), 69, 70
Orbit, 13, 15, 16, 19
  defined, 92

Pacific Plate, 33
"Pacific Ring of Fire," 30
Phenocrysts, 23, 92
Phobos (moon of Mars), 76
Pinacate volcanic field (Mexico), 29
Pioneer-Venus spacecraft, 58, 59, 61,
  63, 64
Planets, 10–12, 13, 14, 15–17, 19
  defined, 92
  See also names of planets
Plate tectonics, 30, 33, 64, 86, 92
Plateau basalts, 28, 92
Pluto (planet), 12, 17, 18, 88
Pumice, 23, 92
Pyroclastic deposits, 26–28, 42, 62, 63,
  92
Pyroxene, 22

Radar, defined, 92
Radar altimeter, 58, 61, 64, 92
Red Spot (Jupiter), 17, 83

Reflectance spectrophotometry, 77
Rhea Mons (Venus), 61
Rilles, 38, 40, 92
Rock samples from Earth's Moon, 42–49
Rocks
  intrusive, 34, 91
  volcanic, 21–23, 42–49, 62

St. Helens, Mount (Washington), 8, 9, 28
Satellites, 92
  Galilean, 83, 91
  natural, 17, 92
Saturn (planet), 10, 14, 17, 18, 86
Scarps, 38, 92
Schmitt, Jack, 47
Shield volcanoes, 24, 25, 38, 61, 63, 65, 68, 69, 70, 71, 74, 85, 92
SNC meteorites, 80, 86, 92
Solar system
  defined, 92
  guide to the, 13–19
Solidification, defined, 92
Spacecraft, 12, 19, 35, 37, 40, 49, 50, 55, 58, 61–63, 65–66, 72–74, 75, 80, 83, 87–89
Spectrophotometry, reflectance, 77

Star, defined, 92
Sun, 13, 15, 92

Tambora (Sumbawa), 9
Theia Mons (Venus), 61
Titan (satellite of Saturn), 86
Titan/Centaur rocket, 10, 11

Uranus (planet), 12, 17, 18, 88

Valles Marineris (Mars), 67
Venera spacecraft (Russia), 61, 62
Vent, defined, 92
Venus (planet), 10, 12, 15, 18, 55, 56–64, 86, 89
Vesicles, 23, 44, 47, 72, 74, 79, 92
Vesta (asteroid), 80
Viking Landers 1 and 2, 72–74
Volcanoes
  active, locations of, 30, 31
  defined, 92
  types of, 24–28
Voyager 1 spacecraft, 83
Voyager 2 spacecraft, 84

Wrinkle ridges, 41, 54, 71, 92

Young, John, 42, 88

87-357

551.2 Taylor, G. Jeffrey
TAY
    Volcanoes in our
    solar system

DATE